Musical Instruments

Drums

By Nick Rebman

level 1 little blue readers

www.littlebluehousebooks.com

Little Blue House is distributed by North Star Editions:
sales@northstareditions.com | 888-417-0195

Produced for Little Blue House by Red Line Editorial.

Photographs ©: Shutterstock Images, cover, 4, 7, 8–9, 11, 12–13, 14–15, 16–17, 24 (top right), 24 (bottom left), 24 (bottom right); iStockphoto, 19, 20–21, 22–23, 24 (top left)

Library of Congress Control Number: 2022910617

ISBN
978-1-64619-698-2 (hardcover)
978-1-64619-730-9 (paperback)
978-1-64619-791-0 (ebook pdf)
978-1-64619-762-0 (hosted ebook)

Printed in the United States of America
Mankato, MN
012023

About the Author

Nick Rebman is a writer and editor who lives in Minnesota. He enjoys reading, walking his dog, and playing rock songs on his drum set.

Table of Contents

I Play the Drums

I play the drums.

I like to make music.

I play the drums.

I use my sticks.

stick

I play the drums.

I move my arms.

arm

I play the drums.

I move my foot.

foot

I play the drums.

I have a teacher.

teacher

I play the drums.

I learn to play a beat.

I play the drums.
I learn to read
sheet music.

sheet music

I play the drums.

I practice every day.

I play the drums.

I wear earplugs.

earplug

I play the drums.

I am in a band.

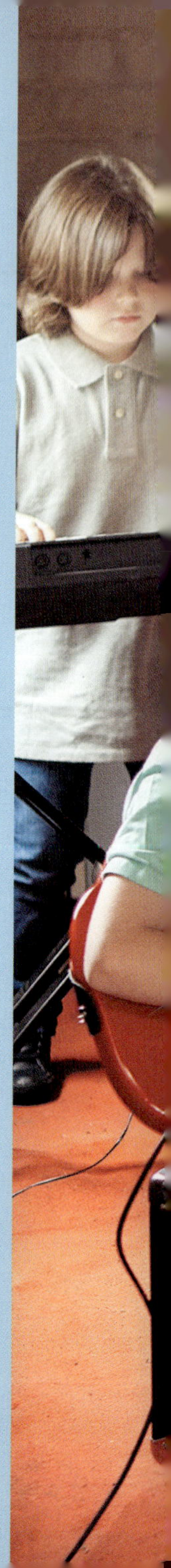

band

Glossary

band

sticks

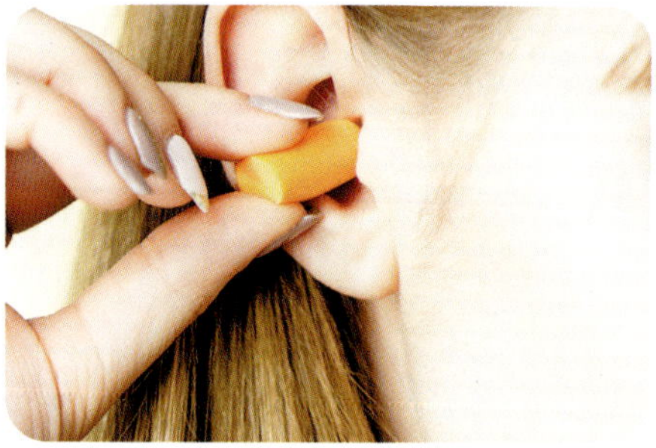

earplug

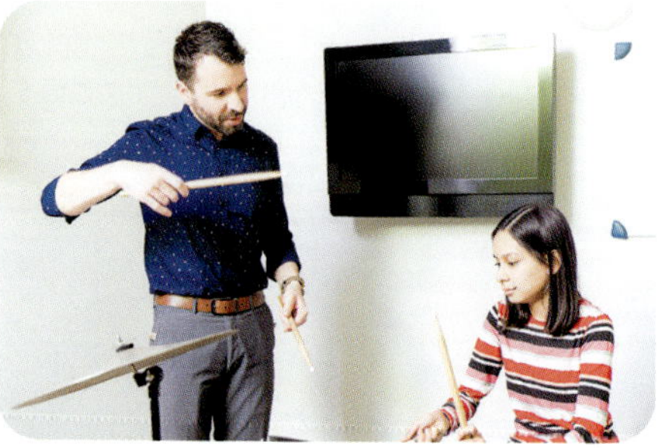

teacher

Index